BREAKOUT BIOGRAPHIES

JUSTIN TRUDEAU

Canadian Prime Minister and Leader of the Liberal Party

Caitie McAneney

New York

Published in 2018 by The Rosen Publishing Group, Inc.
29 East 21st Street, New York, NY 10010

First Edition

Editor: Elizabeth Krajnik
Book Design: Tanya Dellaccio

Photo Credits: Cover Samir Hussein/WireImage/Getty Images; p. 5 Drew Angerer/Getty Images News/ Getty Images; p. 7 (top) Bettmann/Getty Images; p. 7 (bottom) Keystone/Hulton Archive/Getty Images; p. 9 (top) Pool/Getty Images News/Getty Images; p. 9 (bottom) meunierd/Shutterstock.com; p. 11 ROBERTO SCHMIDT/AFP/Getty Images; p. 13 Alfred Eisenstaedt/The LIFE Picture Collection/ Getty Images; p. 15 (top) Colin McConnell/Toronto Star/Getty Images; p. 15 (bottom) Bloomberg/ Getty Images; pp. 17 (top), 19 (bottom), 21 (both) NICHOLAS KAMM/AFP/Getty Images; p. 17 (bottom) arindambanerjee/Shutterstock.com; p. 19 (top) Stacey Newman/Shutterstock.com; p. 23 Carlos Osorio/ Toronto Star/Getty Images; p. 25 (top) Lucas Oleniuk/Toronto Star/Getty Images; p. 25 (bottom) LARS HAGBERG/AFP/Getty Images; p. 27 Nathan Denette/Associated Press/AP Images; p. 29 (top) Spencer Platt/Getty Images News/Getty Images; p. 29 (bottom) ALICE CHICHE/AFP/Getty Images.

Library of Congress Cataloging-in-Publication Data

Names: McAneney, Caitie, author.
Title: Justin Trudeau : Canadian prime minister and leader of the Liberal
  Party / Caitie McAneney.
Description: New York : PowerKids Press, 2018. | Series: Breakout biographies
  | Includes index.
Identifiers: LCCN 2017030210| ISBN 9781538325513 (library bound) | ISBN
  9781538326213 (pbk.) | ISBN 9781538326220 (6 pack)
Subjects: LCSH: Trudeau, Justin. | Prime ministers–Canada–Biography. |
  Canada–Politics and government–1980- | Liberal Party of
  Canada–Biography.
Classification: LCC F1034.3.T78 M35 2018 | DDC 971.07/4092 [B] –dc23
LC record available at https://lccn.loc.gov/2017030210

Manufactured in the United States of America

CPSIA Compliance Information: Batch #BW18PK For Further Information contact Rosen Publishing, New York, New York at 1-800-237-9932

CONTENTS

A PASSIONATE
LEADER

On November 4, 2015, Justin Trudeau took office as the prime minister of Canada. He is the second youngest prime minister in Canadian history. Trudeau has truly broken the mold with his energy, passion for change, and ability to welcome and give a voice to all people.

Trudeau hasn't always been interested in politics. He started his career as a teacher and decided that he could help create more positive change as a politician. Since being elected prime minister, Trudeau has made great strides in creating a better Canada—and a better world.

Even though being prime minister wasn't Trudeau's original plan, it may have been his destiny. During a state visit to Canada in 1972, when Trudeau was just four months old, U.S. President Richard Nixon said: "I'd like to toast the future prime minister of Canada: to Justin Pierre Trudeau."

Trudeau is an engaging and appealing speaker who connects with audiences all over the world.

TRUE SON OF CANADA

Trudeau's family has lived in Canada since 1659. Some say Justin Trudeau is part of a political **dynasty** in Canada. He is the son of Pierre Trudeau, who served as prime minister from 1968 to 1979 and from 1980 to 1984.

Justin Trudeau is the oldest son of Pierre Trudeau and Margaret Sinclair. He was born on December 25, 1971, in Ottawa, Canada. His mother and father had two more sons before they separated and divorced. Pierre raised all three of his sons—Justin, Alexandre or "Sacha," and Michel— while also performing his duties as Canada's prime minister.

In 1984, Pierre resigned, or gave up his position, as prime minister and moved with his sons to Montreal, Canada. There, Justin began attending the Collège Jean-de-Brébeuf. Pierre Trudeau had also attended this school

This photograph taken in 1980 shows Justin (left), Sacha (center), and Michel (right) posing with their father, the prime minister of Canada.

PIERRE TRUDEAU

Pierre Elliott Trudeau was born on October 18, 1919, in Montreal, Quebec. Before serving as prime minister, he was a law professor at the University of Montreal, **parliamentary** secretary to prime minister Lester Pearson, and minister of justice. Pierre Trudeau was known for his casual and offbeat personality and his forward-thinking ideas. As prime minister, he improved Canada's relationship with France and China and was a key part of creating a new Canadian constitution.

COLLEGE YEARS

Trudeau didn't immediately follow in his father's political footsteps. Instead, he decided to study literature at McGill University in Montreal. Trudeau has called himself a "massive reader," saying that he loves to read anything and everything.

When he graduated from McGill University in 1994, Trudeau realized that he wanted to be a teacher. Teaching would give him the opportunity to have a positive impact, or effect, on the world. Trudeau entered the University of British Columbia and graduated in 1998 with a bachelor's degree in education.

For three years, Trudeau taught a number of subjects in schools in Vancouver, British Columbia. He was well liked by his students and loved teaching. However, he had spent a long time on the West Coast of Canada and decided he wanted to go back home to Montreal.

On July 5, 2017, Trudeau received an honorary degree from the University of Edinburgh in Scotland. He was awarded this degree for his achievements as a public servant and his commitment to equality.

MCGILL UNIVERSITY

TRAGEDY FOR THE TRUDEAU FAMILY

Trudeau's early life had been mostly uneventful. However, that would all change in 1998. Trudeau's youngest brother, Michel, died on November 13, 1998. Michel was just 23 years old.

Michel loved the outdoors. He was on a three-day ski trip in Kokanee Glacier Park in British Columbia when an **avalanche** swept him into Kokanee Lake, where he most likely drowned. Trudeau later wrote, "Michel had been doing what he loved most when he died."

Michel's death was a terrible blow to Pierre. While Pierre had been very active for most of his life, his health started to decline after Michel's death. Pierre suffered from **Parkinson's disease** and later, cancer. He decided not to be treated for the cancer, and Justin and Alexandre took care of him until he died on September 28, 2000.

Trudeau and his family said their final goodbyes to Pierre Trudeau during his state funeral in Montreal on October 3, 2000.

BACK IN THE SPOTLIGHT

Trudeau's father's death put him back into the spotlight. Justin was tasked with giving the **eulogy** at his father's funeral. Because Pierre Trudeau was a former prime minister, many important leaders from across Canada and the world were in attendance. The funeral was broadcast on live TV and many people heard Trudeau's graceful and thoughtful words.

In the eulogy, Trudeau told stories about his father that highlighted his strengths as a parent and a champion of individual rights. Trudeau said, "He taught us to believe in ourselves. To stand up for ourselves. To know ourselves, and to accept responsibility for ourselves."

Justin ended the speech with a call to the people of Canada to follow in his father's footsteps. He said it was up to everyone to honor the **legacy** of the former

Justin Trudeau ended his father's eulogy with the simple words "Je t'aime, papa," which means "I love you, father" in French.

COMMITTED
TO SERVICE

Trudeau remained interested in speaking to and teaching young people. He became the chairman of Katimavik, a national youth volunteer program that helps youth from all backgrounds become active citizens. The program encourages young people to do volunteer service for their community to build strong relationships and create positive change. Trudeau believes young people have the power to make a big difference.

During his time as chairman, Trudeau had the opportunity to see firsthand the issues many Canadian youth face. Katimavik had to turn away many applicants because the group didn't have enough funding. Trudeau wanted all young people to have a chance to be active and community-minded citizens and take part in life-changing service. During these years, Trudeau began to uncover his talent for advocacy, or speaking out for others.

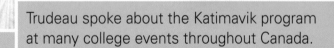

Trudeau spoke about the Katimavik program at many college events throughout Canada.

PRIME MINISTER'S YOUTH COUNCIL

Trudeau's years at Katimavik may have influenced his decision to create the Prime Minister's Youth Council. He formed this council to give young people the opportunity to advise him on national issues that matter most to them. Members of the council have to be between the ages of 16 and 24. They meet online and in person multiple times each year to talk about the concerns of young people in their communities, such as climate change, employment, and education.

STARTING A FAMILY

Sophie Grégoire was a friend and classmate of Trudeau's brother Michel and sometimes played at the Trudeau house as a child. However, Trudeau and Grégoire didn't meet as adults until June 2003, when they cohosted the Mercedes-Benz Grand Prix ball, a fundraiser for the Starlight Children's Foundation. A few months later, Trudeau saw Grégoire again. They got married on May 28, 2005.

Justin and Sophie Trudeau have three children—Xavier, Ella-Grace, and Hadrien. Justin said, "All my life I had wanted more than anything to become a dad. I was inspired by the extraordinary father I'd had, the example he set for me to follow." It's very important to Trudeau that he balances his political life and family life. Trudeau has said that being a father is the best thing in his life.

SOPHIE GRÉGOIRE TRUDEAU

Sophie Grégoire Trudeau was born in Sainte-Adèle, Quebec, on April 24, 1975, and raised in Montreal. She received a degree in communications from McGill University, worked in a newsroom, and then became a TV host on a popular Canadian entertainment show. As the wife of the prime minister, Sophie is very interested in women's rights, equality, and mental health. She became a part of Plan Canada's "Because I Am a Girl" **initiative**. This initiative gives girls around the world the opportunity to get an education and become community leaders.

In an interview with *HuffPost Canada*, Trudeau said on an afternoon off he'd most likely be spending time with his family and he's most proud of his three children.

17

A START
IN POLITICS

Trudeau had settled into life in Montreal. In 2007, he announced that he'd run for a seat in the Canadian Parliament as the Liberal Party's representative for the Papineau riding, or electoral district, in Montreal.

"My career as a politician began in a parking lot," Trudeau has said. He stood with a clipboard outside a grocery store and tried to get people to become members of Canada's Liberal Party. Trudeau hoped to win the nomination for the party and then advance to the election for the Parliament seat. Meeting community members gave Trudeau the opportunity to make connections and learn what people really wanted from the Canadian government.

Trudeau won the nomination and, later, he won the election. He won again in 2011 and 2015. For a person with limited political experience, this was a huge accomplishment.

One of Trudeau's greatest talents is his ability to build strong relationships with citizens and government leaders alike.

THE LIBERAL PARTY

After several years of representing Papineau, Trudeau began campaigning for leadership of Canada's Liberal Party. He said, "Like many Canadian adventures, my campaign for leadership of the Liberal Party began around a campfire." While on a trip to Mont Tremblant in July 2012, Trudeau told a group of close friends, advisers, and family that he realized there were issues that the Canadian government needed to address and that he could be the one to tackle those issues.

Trudeau believed that Canada's government was leaving too many people behind. He promised to help the middle class, build respect for freedom and **diversity**, and create a government that represented *everyone*. Trudeau won the election as the leader of the Liberal Party on April 14, 2013. He has worked to make the Liberal Party more invested in job and skills training, **environmental** initiatives, community building, and civil rights.

Real Change **Now**

Changer ensemble
maintenant

Trudeau's father was also a member of the Liberal Party.

CANADA'S LIBERAL PARTY

There are five main political parties in Canada: the Liberal Party, Conservative Party, Green Party, New Democratic Party, and the Bloc Québécois. Canada's first Liberal government was formed in 1873. Today, the Liberal Party's efforts are directed toward investing in Canada's future through focusing on family care and money for students. The Liberal Party values an open and honest government, helping the middle class, saving the environment, and promoting peace.

Liberal

ACTING
AND BOXING

Trudeau won the support of liberal Canadians through his vision for the country. However, he also won many hearts through his **athleticism**, social media presence, and youthful willingness to do just about anything.

In 2007, Trudeau starred in a TV movie called *The Great War*. He played a real-life hero named Talbot Papineau who fought in World War I. This is the grandson of the man after whom the riding of Papineau is named. *The Great War* was meant to show people Canada's historical role in the war.

On March 31, 2012, Trudeau took part in a celebrity boxing match. He fought Conservative Senator Patrick Brazeau. Trudeau defeated Brazeau in the third round. The event raised more than $230,000, which was donated to the "Fight for the Cure" cancer charity.

Justin Trudeau has taken part in boxing, yoga, skiing, and other activities.

A VOICE FOR THE PEOPLE

On October 19, 2015, Trudeau won reelection. Because the Liberal Party also won control of Parliament in this election, he became prime minister of Canada. His platform of change had spoken to the Canadian people.

Trudeau's mission was to give more voice to citizens. His first step was to pick his cabinet, or the leaders of each government department. Trudeau was the first prime minister to choose a cabinet with an equal number of men and women. His government has granted new funds to women's shelters and started a new investigation into cases where **indigenous** women had been harmed.

Trudeau's government has also given a voice to young people through education grants, or money that is given for a particular purpose, and a national council through which young Canadians can voice their concerns. He's also supported **immigrants** and **refugees**

COMMON GROUND

In 2014, Trudeau published a book about his life, called *Common Ground*. It was released before the 2015 election so Trudeau could define himself before his opponents could. He wanted to show his vision for Canada. The book includes the story of his childhood, his parents' divorce, and his brother Michel's death. Trudeau writes about what he learned from his father during his time as prime minister. He also talks about the importance of the Liberal Party and Conservative Party finding common ground for the sake of the nation.

On April 12, 2017, Trudeau met with Malala Yousafzai, a Pakistani **activist**. She is the youngest person ever to address the Canadian Parliament. In her address, she highlighted issues such as Islamophobia, or the fear or dislike of Islam or people who practice Islam, and women and girls' education throughout the world.

WELCOMING REFUGEES

Trudeau became prime minister as a global crisis, or emergency, was unfolding. People in Syria, a country in the Middle East, were forced to leave their homes because of a deadly civil war. There were many refugees looking for a country that would welcome them.

Trudeau and the Liberal Party promised to accept 25,000 Syrian refugees in 2015. The prime minister welcomed some Syrian refugees at the airport as they arrived in Canada. He passed out winter coats to people who needed them, saying, "You're safe at home now."

In 2017, some leaders from the United States discussed banning refugees from certain countries. Trudeau responded by saying Canada would accept the refugees the United States rejected. He tweeted, "Diversity is our strength."

On December 11, 2015, Trudeau greeted Syrian refugees as they arrived at Pearson International Airport in Toronto. Here, Trudeau poses for photographs with airport workers before greeting refugees.

TRUDEAU'S MESSAGE

Justin Trudeau has focused his role as Canada's prime minister on new ideas and new voices. He is committed to saving the environment, accepting people into Canada, and showing support for diversity. Starting his career as a teacher, Trudeau knows firsthand how important it is to give young people a chance to make a difference.

Trudeau has built upon his father's political legacy as prime minister. He also balances having a family and running a country. Trudeau has carved his own path, bringing Canada into a new age that embraces all peoples and ideas.

In 2016, Trudeau addressed the United Nations, saying, "Every single day, we need to choose hope over fear, and diversity over division." His message is clear: Canada has many voices, but one great mission for change.

Trudeau is known for his great speeches and welcoming attitude.

TIMELINE

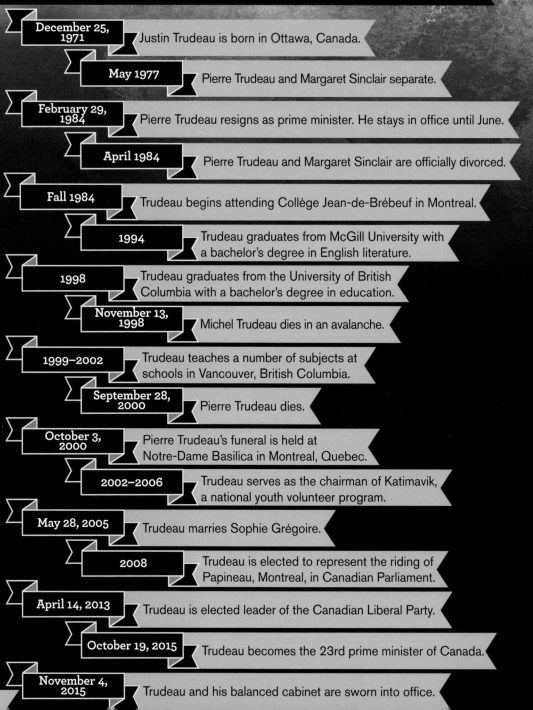

December 25, 1971	Justin Trudeau is born in Ottawa, Canada.
May 1977	Pierre Trudeau and Margaret Sinclair separate.
February 29, 1984	Pierre Trudeau resigns as prime minister. He stays in office until June.
April 1984	Pierre Trudeau and Margaret Sinclair are officially divorced.
Fall 1984	Trudeau begins attending Collège Jean-de-Brébeuf in Montreal.
1994	Trudeau graduates from McGill University with a bachelor's degree in English literature.
1998	Trudeau graduates from the University of British Columbia with a bachelor's degree in education.
November 13, 1998	Michel Trudeau dies in an avalanche.
1999–2002	Trudeau teaches a number of subjects at schools in Vancouver, British Columbia.
September 28, 2000	Pierre Trudeau dies.
October 3, 2000	Pierre Trudeau's funeral is held at Notre-Dame Basilica in Montreal, Quebec.
2002–2006	Trudeau serves as the chairman of Katimavik, a national youth volunteer program.
May 28, 2005	Trudeau marries Sophie Grégoire.
2008	Trudeau is elected to represent the riding of Papineau, Montreal, in Canadian Parliament.
April 14, 2013	Trudeau is elected leader of the Canadian Liberal Party.
October 19, 2015	Trudeau becomes the 23rd prime minister of Canada.
November 4, 2015	Trudeau and his balanced cabinet are sworn into office.

GLOSSARY

activist: Someone who acts strongly in support of or against an issue.

athleticism: The ability to play sports or do physical activities well.

avalanche: A large mass of snow that slides suddenly down a mountain or over a cliff.

diversity: The quality or state of having many different types, forms, or ideas.

dynasty: A succession of leaders from the same family.

environmental: Having to do with the natural world.

eulogy: A speech written in honor of someone who has died.

immigrant: A person who comes to a country to live there.

indigenous: Living naturally in a particular region.

initiative: An act or strategy to improve a situation.

legacy: The lasting effect of a person or thing.

Parkinson's disease: An illness marked by difficulty controlling muscles and balance, which gets worse over time.

parliamentary: Having to do with a parliament, or a group of people who are responsible for making laws in some kinds of government.

refugee: Someone who has been forced to leave a country because of war or for religious or political reasons.

INDEX

WEBSITES

Due to the changing nature of Internet links, PowerKids Press has
developed an online list of websites related to the subject of this book.
This site is updated regularly. Please use this link to access the list: